EARLY AGRICULTURAL MACHINERY

MICHAEL PARTRIDGE

Hugh Evelyn London

First published in 1969
by Hugh Evelyn Limited
9 Fitzroy Square London W1

© 1969 Hugh Evelyn Limited

Designed by Barry Robson
Printed in Great Britain by
Thomas Nelson (Printers) Limited
Bound by W. & J. Mackay & Co Ltd

S.B.N. 238.78820.2.

The author and publishers wish to
acknowledge the invaluable assistance
of Mr S. R. O'Hanlon, MBE in the
preparation of this book. They are
also indebted to Mr L. J. Orvis,
Works Historian of Messrs.
Ransomes, Sims & Jefferies Ltd, for
much useful information and the
loan of illustrated catalogues.

Colour Plates

Engravings

Contents

Introduction

From the primitive farm implements of antiquity to the sophisticated agricultural machines of today is a far cry. Their evolution has been sporadic rather than a smooth progression and not infrequently in the face of scepticism and opposition by farmers and farm workers. Much of it has been trial and error, but gradually the advance has been made until today Britain's agriculture is the most highly mechanised in the world.

Until that great watershed in Britain's history, the Norman Conquest, we have little reliable information about the implements used, literally, to scratch a living from the soil. In very early times we can be sure that the first 'plough' was nothing more than a digging-stick pushed by hand through the soil to leave a shallow depression in which seed could be sown. When later the caschrom, a form of wooden spade operated as a lever by hand and foot, was devised to give greater penetration and some slight inversion of the soil, the concept of the plough had been born. Pulling the implement, first by men and subsequently by domestic animals, was a natural development.

With the coming of the Angles and Saxons after the Roman legions withdrew, the heavy, single-furrow wooden plough, drawn by oxen, is seen as a great advance, primitive as it was. The early harrows, too, dating from the tenth century, were cumbersome wooden affairs – often nothing more than thorn bushes secured to a stout frame.

Instead of the small square fields of Celtic times, the area of land used for cultivation was divided into strips and shared between members of a settlement. The strips were ploughed and the crops grown until the harvest showed signs of diminishing; then fresh land was cleared and cultivated whilst the other piece was given over to the grazing of sheep and cattle. In this manner the fertility of the soil was replenished and the land could later be used as arable again with excellent results.

A regular system of crop rotation thus became established and continued throughout the Middle Ages until, with the introduction of roots and clover in the eighteenth century, more efficient systems were evolved. The new principles laid the foundation of our modern crop husbandry. To make the most of the improved systems and the effects of adequate manuring, the farmer found that more efficient machines and implements were necessary – a view shared and stimulated by the growing number of agricultural societies, who organised demonstrations and competitions for inventions and such other improvements as would lighten the farmer's tasks.

The eighteenth century also saw a remarkable advance in the form of the seed-drill constructed by Jethro Tull and his revolutionary ideas of horse-hoeing, and later the development of threshing and winnowing machines that replaced the ancient flail and the age-old methods of separating grain from chaff. In the same century a wide variety of horse-drawn implements was developed. Important changes in plough design were brought about by theorists like James Small and Arbuthnot, leading ultimately to the mass-production of iron ploughs.

Better harvesting and threshing machinery followed in the next century, but when the potential of steam power was also placed at the farmer's command the horizon of agricultural endeavour was greatly extended. Steam engines that had been used to power barn machinery were re-designed and used with great effect to haul gigantic ploughs and drive the elaborate digging machinery that began to come forward. Steam cultivation reached its peak early in the present century, but by this time the first oil-driven tractors were making their appearance.

So long as the developments in agricultural machinery were circumscribed by the restricted knowledge and capacity of the village smithy and the carpenter's shop, progress was slow, but with the quickening pace of the new industrial era, the making of standard implements and spare parts became possible on a wide scale and the Golden Age of farming had dawned.

SECTION 1

The development of the plough

From the evidence of old manuscripts and drawings it can be seen that throughout the Middle Ages many types of light and heavy ploughs were being used in Britain, some with wheels and some without. During the seventeenth century agricultural writers began to study the design and construction of cultivation implements more closely. One of their main criticisms was that there were too many types of plough in use, varying, as they did, with different parts of the country according to the terrain and nature of the soil. Clearly the time had come when the mechanics of the plough should be examined and some kind of specification laid down as to its general shape and the design of its component parts.

Most ploughs at this time, whether or not they had wheels, were constructed almost wholly of timber; the exceptions were those parts that came in contact with the soil, namely the share (which cuts through the soil prior to turning over by the mould-board) and the coulter (a sharpened length of iron fixed through the beam so as to cut the soil vertically before the share). The

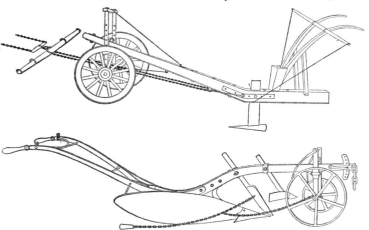

(*top*) Mr. Vaisey's Mole Plough, c 1790 (*below*) Warwickshire Prize Plough, c 1850 (plate 3)

shapes of these particular parts were always a matter of contro-versy. The blacksmiths making them relied on local tradition, designing both share and coulter to such differing patterns as they believed were best suited to particular soils. For hard or stony land a pointed share was thought to be most suitable, but on soft, sticky land one less pointed was preferable. Coulters were made straight or curved and sometimes set in front of the tip of the share and sometimes behind it.

This was the confused state of things in the mid-seventeenth century, when an attempt was made by Walter Blith (1652) to lay down the essentials of good plough design and construction. From his own experiments and practice in the field he set down his recommendations for a better design, commenting that the timber and iron construction of existing ploughs was too heavy and that often the handles were too short or too long to ensure

absolute control. He suggested improvements for the design of the coulter, share and mouldboard in relation to the natural turn of the furrow. Out of his work came a firm foundation upon which future designers and theorists could elaborate.

Ideas and improvements continued to emerge during the remainder of the century, but inventors were cautious, and however ingenious or efficient their developments, no one added anything of significance to Blith's theory of the plough for a century or more after his death.

About 1730 a plough, thought to have originated in Holland, was brought into use near Rotherham, in Yorkshire – a fact which eventually resulted in its being known as the Rotherham plough. It was made of wood and fitted with a share and coulter of iron and an iron-plated mouldboard. It became very popular in both England and Scotland and a great number were made, so marking the first positive step towards British factory plough production. But it was James Small of Berwick who, a little later, first demonstrably applied mathematical principles to plough design and developed the cast-iron curved mouldboard. He believed that the countless patterns of mouldboard in general use could be replaced by a single, universal shape cast in iron, and with this in mind he set about applying mathematics to the plough in order to produce the perfect and practical shape of mouldboard. His plough was a great improvement on the earlier Rotherham and was quickly adopted throughout the North.

The theory and debate which surrounded plough design indicated a desire for improvements in agriculture that was to increase during the eighteenth century, and the competition between designers was intensified by the offer of medals and prizes by societies for outstanding developments. Trials were arranged, both publicly and privately, to determine the merits of one particular plough over another. Ploughing matches were also organised, which had a marked effect in raising the standard of the ploughmen themselves.

The early nineteenth century saw the factory production of ploughs well established. Ransomes had already taken out a number of patents, including one for plough bodies that could easily be dismantled whilst in the field so that new or alternative parts could be bolted on. Other factories were established in England and Scotland, and where manufacturers did not have their own shops they could supply their implements or parts through agents.

In spite of all the activity amongst inventors and manu-facturers, the use of new cast-iron implements did not spread over the country immediately. Farmers, as always, continued to use the implements that they knew and were accustomed to.

SECTION 2

Land drainage

Land which is continuously wet cannot be cultivated successfully until it has been drained. The Romans were well aware of this and, by means of both open and covered drains, brought some parts of Britain under cultivation that had hitherto been marshy wasteland. Their methods were continued by the native Celts after the Romans withdrew from the country, and subsequently by the Anglo-Saxons. But these early attempts were not altogether effective, mainly because of the unsuitability of the materials used in the construction of the drains – usually brushwood and small boulders. These were laid in the bottom of a trench and covered with soil, which served to direct the flow of water. This type of drain had a short life; it easily became choked with silt or collapsed.

Towards the end of the eighteenth century Joseph Elkington, who in 1769 had been given £1,000 by the Board of Agriculture, tackled the problem of wet land by intercepting the water at its source. He located the position of various springs on his land, and by means of a stone-filled trench he effectively led the water from its points of origin into one large main drain. But this system did not solve the greater problem of land that retained the winter rainfall and remained too wet for cultivation until the late spring. Walter Blith was probably the first person to record the use of implements specially designed and constructed for this type of drainage work. These were made in the late seventeenth century and took the form of ploughs with shares capable of cutting deep furrows through which the water could flow away.

A common method of drain construction at this time was to use large, flat stones laid across the bottom of a trench, the sides of which were built up with more stones laid lengthways, and the top covered in by another layer set crosswise. This form of drainage, along with the use of open ditches, remained popular until the turn of the century. Then the draining plough was developed on a larger sacle.

During the 1760's a Mr Knowles and a Mr Cuthbert Clarke were both awarded prizes by the Royal Society of Arts for the construction of a practical draining implement. Clarke's plough was built of heavy wooden beams which carried a divided roller at the front end. The function of the roller was to prevent the coulters from penetrating too deeply into the soil, but the implement was too heavy to work properly. Knowles's plough

was equally unsuccessful and rejected after some two dozen had been made. Similar types of plough had probably been used for many years before the Royal Society's competition. The Cambridge draining plough, for example, excavated a trench 12 in. deep and 18 in. wide, and needed a team of twenty horses to draw it. This plough was the basis of most of the designs produced at that time.

During the eighteenth century tile drainage came into favour. This comprised semi-circular bricks resting on the flat bottom of a trench to form an arch: alternatively, they could be used to form an open gulley or be used in pairs to make a closed pipe. Along with the perfection of brick- and tile-making machinery, the manufacture of a cylindrical clay pipe was achieved by John Reade, a gardener who made a number of 1-in. diameter pipes for the purpose of heating a conservatory. He made his first pipes by hand, bending a sheet of clay around a wooden shaft and working it smooth with water. The possibility of using such pipes in land drainage quickly became apparent. The bore of the pipes was increased and a machine was designed (by Thomas Scragg) to produce as many as 20,000 pipes a day.

Patents for mole ploughs had already been taken out, but the development of this implement had been delayed by the attention given to tile drainage. Mole drainage was a satisfactory alternative and indeed had the considerable advantage of saving both time and labour, but it was suitable only for clay and heavy soils. The pointed cylindrical 'mole' of about 3-in. diameter was attached to a narrow coulter and set to the depth of drain required. The mole was then dropped into the soil and, as the plough was hauled, it left channels underground which terminated at a suitably situated permanent tile drain.

The general interest aroused in land drainage improvements was responsible for a notable invention by a Scotsman named James Smith of Deanston – the subsoil plough. In 1823 Smith took over a 189-acre farm on poor quality soil, wet and partly covered with rushes. His first attempt at improving the land was by means of parallel field drains laid at a depth of 2½ ft, with the main drains laid at 4 ft and the receiving drains at 3 ft. This network, which covered the entire area of his land, was filled to within 18 in. of the surface with boulders and stone fragments. These drains proved to be effective, but it occurred to Smith that if the tight subsoil could be broken up without being mixed into the upper layer, as happened when the common trench plough was used, the water would be able to filter through into the drains more easily. It was for this purpose that he invented his subsoil plough, an implement of great weight that penetrated the soil to a depth of 16 in. and effectively worked the sterile subsoil without bringing it up.

The results of Smith's effort to combine subsoiling and underground drainage proved outstanding. He and his farm became famous when neighbours saw for themselves the vast

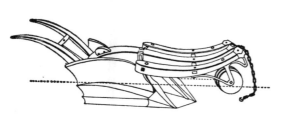

Cuthbert Clarke's Draining Plough, c 1760 (plate 16

improvements he had made. The news spread throughout Scotland and England, and he was inundated with visitors who wished to see the thriving garden that was once sour, water-logged land. To this he added the refinement of collecting and pumping the water in measured quantities. Many farmers began to imitate his method, and they too saw a vast improvement in their own crops. The subsoil plough immediately became popular, and improved versions were constructed and sold by various manufacturers.

Then came John Fowler's famous mole draining plough, which he exhibited at the Great Exhibition of 1851. This was a massive timber affair, hauled by a capstan turned by horses and designed to lay a long string of short wooden pipes, threaded on a wire rope, at a depth of up to four feet. At the end of the run the wire was detached and pulled clear, so leaving the pipes to form a completed drain.

A rotary digging machine, designed to lighten the task of trenching, was the invention of a Mr Paul, a Norfolk gentleman, in the 1850's. This also was hauled by capstan and horses. It comprised a heavy chassis into which was set a huge wheel, with digging tines set around the perimeter. A hole was dug out by hand and the machine, positioned to the required depth, was driven by chain from a turning capstan.

Machines were developed to open drains, lay the pipes and replace the soil in a single operation. Amongst these was one made by Robson and Hardman in 1880 that took the form of two endless chains of buckets set in tandem. This heavy machine was powered by a steam engine, and the turning of the land-wheels was transmitted through gear-wheels to turn the bucket chains. As the soil was raised in the buckets, the drain pipes were fed down from inside the machine. Such large machines were usually worked by contractors, since the capital outlay was too great for the average farmer.

The function of the harrow is to create a tilth in which seeds can be sown and/or covered, and to remove some of the less noxious weeds. The nineteenth century harrow consisted of four longitudinal timber bars with five iron teeth, or tines, driven at intervals into each bar. The frame was held stable by cross-bars which passed over the longitudinal bars and were secured by pegs. So that each tine should not follow in the same track as the one in front of it, the harrow was drawn by harnessing the horse at one corner. This diagonal pull thus threw the tines into a sidelong movement and each left its own separate track. Harrows of this nature were usually worked in pairs. To prevent them from coming together, a cross-tie was bolted over the two, so keeping them equidistant and ensuring that neither would rise from the ground.

Although the iron harrow appeared at the beginning of the nineteenth century, it did not attract much attention. Repairs were not so easily or cheaply carried out as they were on the timber implement, and because of its weight it was also more difficult to manoeuvre than the timber harrow. Nevertheless, by the use of iron, makers were able to develop a sectional zig-zag form (in which the tines were staggered), so allowing the implement to be trailed in a straight line. Sections were also arranged side by side, which permitted each individual section to rise and fall with the irregularities of the ground.

Broken tines were a constant problem on stony ground, and it was a welcome improvement, therefore, when J. & F. Howard obtained a patent for fitting tines into the harrow more securely. The holes in the upper beam were screw-tapped and a corresponding thread was put into the tine, so that the whole implement was firm. Replacement tines could now be fitted more easily and quickly.

Grass-seed harrows were a smaller, lighter form of the field harrow and had a multitude of fine, sharp teeth which served the delicate purpose of covering the grass seed with a fine tilth.

An implement similar to the harrow was the grubber, a tool contrived to serve the double purpose of ploughing and harrowing. It was, in fact, subsidiary to both plough and harrow and never a complete substitute for either. Weight and strength were necessary in order that it could pierce the earth and withstand the power of a horse team. It was constructed wholly of wrought-iron. The frame, with curved pointed prongs, was suspended on an axle. Two wheels, adjustable for height, were at the rear, and a third wheel was placed at the front for steering.

The scarifier was similar in appearance to the grubber, but had a triangular frame on three small iron wheels. A lever lifted or lowered the frame of teeth to a suitable depth for working. Though light in construction, this implement was most useful for clearing land fouled with weeds.

During the actual growing season of the crop the farmers' efforts were concentrated on controlling weed growth, and in the early years the only methods available were hand pulling or slashing off the tops with a sickle. The simple, but effective, horse-hoe was developed in order to hoe between rows of growing crops and remove the weeds. It was not an improved version of any earlier implement, but an entirely new idea in husbandry

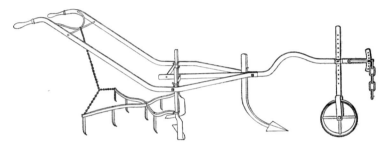

Horse Drawn Hoe, 1860 (plate 6)

practice brought about by Jethro Tull. The frame of the horse-hoe was made of iron, with a single wheel at the front which regulated the share penetration. The side-cutters were made to slide on the frame so as to match the width required, admitting variation of some 14–24 in. An expanding harrow could be attached to the rear, which was helpful in bringing weeds to the surface of the soil. The implement, carefully guided by the operator from the rear, was light enough to be pulled by one horse.

At the beginning of the nineteenth century, rollers were being used increasingly in the cultivation of green crops, where soil had to be reduced to a finer texture than the plough or harrow could make it. The rollers themselves were made to various patterns and sizes, usually of iron and weighted with stones to increase the pressure. Rollers could be obtained either plain or spiked, and a miniature model, weighing about 6 cwt, was available. They were extremely useful for the lighter tasks, such as rolling sown ridged crops.

Clod crushers looked very much like rollers, but were furnished with sharp or serrated rims which cut and broke the clods as well as crushing them. The Cambridge clod crusher was composed of a number of iron discs which revolved independently on an axle. The sharp, narrow rims penetrated to good effect on heavy clay, since the implement cut the lumps into segments, whereas the plain roller tended only to compress them.

An outstandingly original cultivating machine was evolved in 1857 by Messrs Blackburn of Derby. The chief feature of this 7-ton machine was a huge corrugated drum that crushed the clods. A harrow drawn from the rear broke down the soil even more. The chassis comprised big wooden beams, and the drum, made of ½-in.-thick steel plate, had a corrugated circumference 6 ft wide. The vertical boiler set within the drum supplied steam to the engine cylinders. Steering was governed by a horizontal hand-wheel mounted on the footplate, above a small fore-carriage. The manufacturers advertised the machine as having a bearing load per square inch of less than that of a horse's hoof. As a crusher only, 40 acres could be worked in a single day, but with a harrow attached the amount of work was cut by half. Six specially constructed ploughs could be attached and hauled at a speed of 3 m.p.h. When unburdened and on a good surface the machine could achieve a speed of 6 m.p.h.

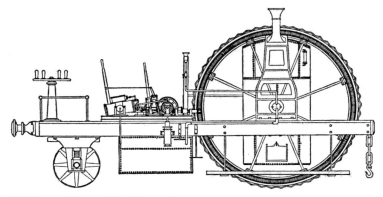

Blackburn Digger, 1857 (plate 10)

SECTION 4

The seed drill

Although credit is usually given to Jethro Tull for inventing the first seed-drill, it is now known that a primitive implement for the same purpose was used by the Chinese about 2500 B.C. This is thought to have been a wheelbarrow type of construction, with a hopper and funnels to distribute the seeds. Various types of drill were almost certainly used by the Romans, and in post-medieval times Italy can claim an early patent for a seed-drill taken out by a Venetian, Camillo Torello, in 1566.

By the seventeenth century British inventors had experimented with a number of ideas for dropping seeds into the soil, some of which were described in the books and literature of the time. One such notable book, titled *Briefe Discoveries of Divers Excellent Wayes and Means for the Improving and Manuring of Land*, by J. Sha (1646), describes a machine designed to sow seeds and manure simultaneously. Apparently it had three funnels for dropping the seeds and two for the manure. The seeds would be dropped into the required depth of soil and the manure applied sparingly into the same furrow. There is, however, no indication whether this machine was ever built and tried.

Another design claimed as a practical instrument for sowing seed was described by John Worlidge in his book *Systema Agriculturae* (1669). The seed-dropping device on this machine was to prove an important contribution. It consisted of a wooden wheel with leather projections which, when turned by a belt from the rear wheels, caught the seeds and delivered them into a wooden pipe through which they fell to the soil. This was a basic type of force-feed drill; an alternative method of seeding was the spoon-feed drill, invented later by a German named Locatelli. In this machine the seed and the dropping device were in separate compartments. The dropping mechanism consisted of four rows of metal spoons fixed into a thick wooden axle. When the axle was turned by the land-wheels, the spoons caught the seeds in the bottom of their box and tossed them into funnels, whence they fell to the ground. This drill was attached to a plough and the seed sown immediately after the plough had opened up the soil. Its outstanding feature was the seed-dropping device, the principle of which has remained until the present time.

It is unlikely that any of these early attempts at seed-drilling ever reached practical application, and so the machine made by Tull can still be acclaimed the first to work effectively. Jethro Tull (1674-1741) was an Oxford graduate who, because of bad health, went to live in Berkshire. It is thought that he produced his machine for seeding in rows as a direct result of his enthusiasm for his cultivation and horse-hoeing techniques. He based his first drill on the shape of a wheelbarrow and followed it with several variations, but he kept a similar pattern for the seed-dropper, which was a revolving cylinder with regularly spaced holes that caught the seeds from the hopper above and dropped them into the open furrows.

The drill that Tull devised could sow three rows of seed and was light enough to be drawn by a single horse. It was constructed almost entirely of timber and was carried on four wheels, two large ones at the front and smaller ones at the rear. The large

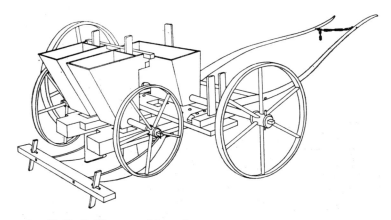

Jethro Tull's Drill, c 1700 (plate 4)

wheels carried a seed hopper and dropping device on their axle to feed the centre coulter, and the smaller wheels carried two hoppers and mechanism to feed the outer coulters. The coulters or hoes were arranged so as to pierce the soil below the machine and each had a channel cut into the back which directed the falling seed into the soil. Control of the flow of the seed past the notched cylinder was achieved by means of a thin metal plate and a spring.

The practice of drilling, which enabled a farmer to sow in parallel lines and at any width he chose, was clearly in the interests of better farming, and many types of seed-drill were devised. Some were simple, but the majority were heavy and over-complicated. Not surprisingly, therefore, opposing schools of thought continued to exist as to whether dibbling or drilling produced the higher yields.

The dibbling method involved in the controversy was one that seems to have had little advantage over spiking-out holes by hand. This method employed a setting board about 4 ft long drilled with holes at regular intervals. The board was placed alongside a guide rope and a dibber was pushed through each hole in turn. The dibber was furnished with a projection which prevented it from going too far through the board and so ensured holes of uniform depth, into which the seed was subsequently dropped. But however excellent this method was thought to be, it must have been very tiring for the labourer, who was continually bending or kneeling as he worked across the field.

George Winter, of Charlton, Gloucestershire, designed and made a seed-drill which had spiked wheels and a wide selection of slotted cylinders to accommodate a variety of seed sizes. The required size of cylinder was fixed to the axle inside the bottom of the seed hopper which, when turned, passed the seeds, via channels in the coulters, down to the soil. The seed fell continuously with each revolution of the land-wheels.

Despite the variety of seed-drills available, they did not come into general use for some time. For example, in parts of Kent farmers were loath to discontinue the use of the 'striking plough', an implement that cut channels into which the seed was cast by hand, then harrowed into rows. Seed-drills were used in Suffolk, but the accepted and growing method of sowing a field in this part of the country was by the drill roller, the function of which was to leave numerous parallel channels across the land, into which the seed was cast.

In 1782 the Reverend James Cooke patented a spoon-feed drill which was to prove an important development because its principle was used and built upon by later inventors. His own particular drill was improved upon a few years later by Henry Baldwin and Samuel Wells. This provided a longer axle and adjustable wheels which allowed for the addition of more dropping cups and coulters. There was also a device which allowed each coulter to ride independently and adjust itself to an irregular soil surface. Many of these improved machines were made and sold, but to contractors rather than farmers.

It was in Suffolk at the end of the eighteenth century that a development took place that was to have a deep and long-lasting effect on farmers in Britain. It was due to James Smyth, a wheelwright, who was frequently called upon by the local farmers to repair drills and other implements. Together with his brother he devised a method of making the drill coulters individually adjustable to differing widths (the Norfolk drill, with fixed coulters, was normally used in that area). The type of machine they built was a combined seed- and manure-drill, with a gear-drive similar to Cooke's earlier machine. It also had a method of steering which enabled the operator to swing the coulters to the left or right in order to keep the sowing lines straight and true.

This machine achieved remarkable popularity, for the Smyths were not content to provide merely for the nearby farmers; they demonstrated it over a wide area and undertook seed-drilling on a contract basis. This became a highly successful venture and the firm expanded quickly.

By this time two types of drill had established themselves – the cup-feed and the force-feed. Many carried an additional hopper for manure that fell along with the seed. There were numerous varieties of simple one-row drill barrows, used for sowing peas, beans and turnip seed, as well as machines for the 'broadcast' distribution of small seeds, such as clover.

The broadcast seed-drill sowed seeds over a wide area and consisted of a narrow box 15–16 ft long, holding the seed, which

was carried on a wheelbarrow-type of frame. An iron spindle running along the entire length of the box revolved and threw out the seeds from holes in the box by means of hair brushes or knobs of wood attached to the spindle, one opposite each hole. A strip of brass controlled by a screw was used to adjust the size of the outlet and so regulate the amount of seed being cast. The machine was drawn by one horse, and the operator followed holding the handles of the chassis. From this position it was possible for him to see the work being done and to replenish the seed when necessary.

In a later version of this implement the long seed box was made to fold, which facilitated transport between farm and fields. It was divided into three sections, the centre section about 9 ft long and the outer ones, which folded to the middle, 4½ ft long.

In 1839 a drop-drill with spacing mechanism was produced,

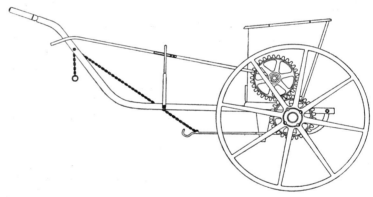

One-Row Seed Drill, c 1900 (plate 8)

with which it was possible to drop seeds and manure at desired intervals – and not only in a continuous stream as hitherto. Regulating was by means of valves which were opened at calculated intervals by a studded wheel turning on the main axle. The valve closed immediately after the stud passed it, and in this way the seed and manure could be dropped at the required spacing.

A great number of seed-drills were shown and demonstrated at the agricultural trials of the mid-nineteenth century; no other machine had experienced such widespread development in so short a time. Manufacturers could be found in almost every county, but all their machines were variations of the same principle. By the 1860's seed-drills had become firmly established in their design, and they have changed very little since.

SECTION 5

Haymaking machinery

Little or no attempt to mechanise haymaking was made before the nineteenth century. Cutting, gathering and stacking were done entirely by hand, as they had been from time immemorial. When Robert Salmon of Woburn made his haymaking machine, or tedder, very early in the 1800's, farmers were quick to see its advantages. Field-work was speeded up and the turning of the grass was done much more efficiently. This machine, which was to be the prototype of later tedders, was of simple construction, with a main axle and two large ground wheels. To the same axle were attached two smaller wheels, the outer edges of which were connected with wooden battens, thus forming a horizontal cylinder around the main axle. Iron spikes were fixed into the battens, so that when the machine was drawn across the meadow the cylinder revolved and the spikes caught, lifted and tossed the hay.

This machine was used mainly in the London area after 1830, but it was improved upon some ten years later by a Mr. Wedlake, of Hornchurch, Essex. He split the cylinder into two independent sections and supported the iron spikes on springs, so that if they should happen to catch any solid object they would give way before resuming their proper position. But the operator had little control over the effects caused by the machine. When tossed in the air the hay could sail a long distance on the wind and however widely scattered had eventually to be raked together by hand. What was now needed was a simple horse-rake, and such an implement, mainly used for clearing bean stubble, did in fact already exist. By adjusting the spacing of its tines, here was a ready-made machine that could reduce hand labour considerably.

A semi-mechanised pattern thus began to emerge, but the routine of the day's work remained largely unchanged. The hay tedder was used to scatter the crop in the early morning, and this would be left in the sun for the remainder of the day. Then the horse-rake would be used to collect it into rows and the hay-cocks built by hand before the evening.

An efficient horse-drawn drag-rake was made by Smith & Ashby at this time. It was a version of the hand drag-rake which in its simplest form was a large wooden rake about 4 ft 6 in. wide, with steel teeth, used to collect loose corn. Smith & Ashby mounted a wider version across an axle with two large wheels. Each tine was curved towards the front and made to swing independently.

A drag-rake sold by Ransomes won first prize at the Royal Agricultural Society's Show at Salisbury in 1857. This was an iron machine with light steel teeth. Each tooth was independently sprung, so that the whole set readily adjusted itself to uneven land. The frame had side levers so that the rake could be used and kept level, even with one wheel running in a deep furrow. An arc on the shafts enabled the teeth to be set either to penetrate the ground or to skim the surface lightly, thus preventing soil or rubbish from being collected with the hay. Each alternate tooth could be raised out of work when desired and so form a coarse rake; this was a useful device when raking twitch or other difficult weeds.

Smith & Ashby were amongst the first manufacturers to produce a really efficient haymaker. It was similar to Wedlake's machine where the revolving rake was divided into independent sections to resist obstructions, but improved inasmuch that the sections were thrown out of gear if the machine was turned or reversed.

Between 1840 and 1850 the development of haymaking machines went ahead rapidly. Numerous implements were designed and patented; trials and demonstrations were continually being held, and money prizes given to the winners. Manufacturers at this time were not slow to display on the covers of their catalogues the facsimilies of medals, rosettes and certificates which had been awarded to them for various achievements. New firms sprang up to design, manufacture and market haymaking machinery, and the older established firms were also producing such machines.

Nicholson's patent double-action haymaking machine, which cost sixteen guineas in the mid-nineteenth century, won first prize in its section at Salisbury in 1857. It worked on a similar principle to that of the earlier machines, except that the whole construction was of iron and finely balanced. This implement threw the crop easily and was calculated to do the work of some 16–20 adult labourers. When such machines were in motion, however, much inconvenience was caused by the flying hay which tended to smother both horse and implement. To minimise this handicap, Ashby, Jefferey and Lake devised a canvas hood to cover the front of their machine, which had the additional benefit of reducing clogging in the mechanism. The idea of using a hood was adopted by most manufacturers, but light metal was used in preference to canvas.

The Haseley tedder, or kicker, was demonstrated in 1889 and represented an attempt to smooth out the violent jerking experienced with other machines. It was fitted with a number of spring forks that worked by crankshafts from the land-wheels and kicked out from the rear of the machine. This was the type of implement that found favour during the latter part of the nineteenth century and was manufactured by a number of firms. The haykicker was very soon replaced by the swath turner, which was perfected along with the side delivery rake in the early years of the present century.

Hay presses were manufactured in the USA before 1850, since two Americans, P. K. Dederick and George Emery, had increasingly given their attention to the development of such a machine. Portable balers became established in America by the 1870's, and in 1882 Dederick's hay press made its appearance in Britain. It was known as the 'perpetual press' and was capable

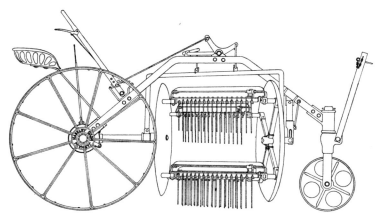

Combined Swath Turner and Side Delivery Rake, Jarmain, c 1920 (plate 7)

of baling and tying straw into a solid block. Loose straw was fed continuously through a hopper to a closed area below, where it was pulled down by a wooden arm and held fast by spring levers until compressed into a bale. It was then tied by wire and ejected from the rear of the machine.

Mechanical hay-loaders, which can still be seen in various stages of decay about the countryside, were developed and perfected in the latter part of the nineteenth century.

SECTION 6

Patrick Bell and the reaping machine

Outstanding among the features of the nineteenth century was the perfection of the reaping machine and its subsequent evolution into the reaper and binder. It was widely doubted whether a successful corn reaper could ever be constructed; to be able to cut corn without loss or damage seemed quite impracticable. From time immemorial the sickle and the scythe had been the established tools, notwithstanding that the Romans had a cart-like machine which was pushed by an ox into the standing corn. The leading edge of the cart was fitted with teeth which cut or tore off the heads of grain which were then passed into the cart by the accompanying worker.

The first patent for a reaping machine was granted to Joseph Boyce, of London, in 1800. The principle involved a horizontal rotating disc which had several small scythes attached to the rim. But this reaper was only partially successful, since its performance proved unreliable.

Thomas James Plucknett, of Deptford, an experienced agricultural engineer, presented his version of the reaper in 1805. He employed a sharpened circular plate with notched edges which revolved horizontally and was adjusted for cutting height. The corn stalks were directed into the fine-toothed disc which cut extremely well, but no provision was made for the machine to collect the corn. This idea was elaborated upon by Gladstones, of Kirkcudbright, who employed a cutting disc similar to Plucknett's, driven from the land-wheels by belts. The corn was gathered and held into the cutting disc by forks which rotated on the same axle. The machine incorporated a self-sharpening device.

One reaping machine that received favourable reports at official trials was that designed and built by James Smith, of Deanston. Here again the cutter was of circular form, but this time it was attached to and projected a little beyond the base of a vertical drum that turned on its axis. When it was pushed forward by horses, the drum and its cutter were turned by a shaft and gears from the ground-wheels. The corn, being cut away near the roots, fell against the drum and was deposited alongside the machine in a continuous row. This machine won prizes and was regarded as having great potential, but unfortunately, due to lack of encouragement, Smith abandoned it. Both Gladstone's and Smith's ideas were incorporated in subsequent reaping machines, some of them by amateur inventors.

An original design came from Joseph Mann, of Cumberland, in 1820. He obtained support for his idea from the Abbey Holme Agricultural Society, whose well-intentioned suggestions unfortunately held back developments. Mann abandoned his machine but later undertook to improve upon it, and his resulting machine cut satisfactorily, but on flat ground only. It had a triangular chassis with a twelve-sided cutter geared to one of the three land-wheels. The corn was gathered and held on to the cutters by revolving rakes, after which it was stripped from the

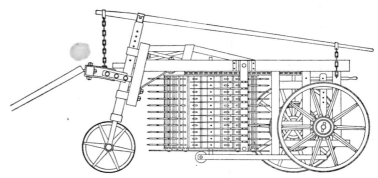

Mann's Reaping Machine, c 1830 (plate 1)

rakes and laid in a regular swath alongside the machine.

New methods and improvements were tried but, in the absence of any real encouragement, were abandoned after little success, and for some time hardly any progress was made. Any machine constructed about this time had a fairly short life – except, however, the reaper designed by Patrick Bell. This machine was designed to survive for many years, and indeed some of Bell's ideas can still be found in the reaper-binders of the twentieth century.

Patrick Bell, born in 1801, was one of a large farming family, and after studying divinity at St Andrews he became minister to a small parish in his home county of Angus. He was, however, mechanically minded and must have seen during his early life the difficulties of assembling the labour and equipment needed to harvest the extensive acreage of Scottish oats and barley. At the time he began to construct his machine he had already seen an engraving of Smith's earlier attempt. Bell's idea for the cutters came from an ordinary pair of garden shears, and his notion that mechanical clippers would prove more effective than mechanical scythes was to provide the basis of his reaper. He fixed one half of the triangular shear blades on to a bar at regular intervals, and this bar was geared to the land-wheels which provided a reciprocating motion. The other blades he fixed to a stationary bar, so that a cutting action was secured when the blades came together. As the machine advanced, the crop was brought and held fast to the cutters by means of revolving sails, very similar to those of the modern combine harvester. The cut corn was delivered alongside the machine by a travelling canvas, which was also turned by gearing from the land-wheels.

Bell tried out his new machine secretly in a closed barn, using for the experiment part of a crop of oats taken from a field and replanted one by one in the earth floor. The next trial took place at night during the autumn of 1828. This time Bell was assisted by his brother. The trial was a success and, as a result, his reaping machine was publicly demonstrated; it continued to work well and some half-dozen more were made. Because of poor workmanship, however, they lasted for only one season. More capable builders undertook to make stronger models, sometimes adding their own 'improvements'. Bell had deliberately neglected to take out a patent in order that his reaping machine could be brought into general use at as low a cost as possible, but with no patent protecting his machine the inventor was unable to dispute the various modifications brought into its construction. Individual carpenters and wheelwrights were free to produce their own doubtful versions of the original.

The introduction of any implement that replaced hand labour was greatly resented by the farm workers at this period, and it was at about this time that they rose in rebellion against the new mechanical threshing machine. Patrick Bell's original reaper was maintained by his brother who farmed his own land at Inchmichael, in Perthshire. He used the machine annually, replacing or strengthening the weakest parts. By 1832 ten machines had been built, of which two were sent to Poland and two to Australia. During these years the Bell brothers were giving advice and instruction on the proper management of the reaping machine, and farmers in the locality of Inchmichael became well acquainted with its mechanism. Many such men were to leave Scotland for America and undoubtedly took some knowledge of the reaping machine with them. No reaper was ever sent to America from Britain, but it is probable that the experiences related by the incoming farmers, along with written reports on Bell's reaper, influenced the American inventors, whose machines caused a sensation when shown at the Great Exhibition at the Crystal Palace in 1851. It was through this exhibition and the showing of the American reapers, designed by McCormick and Hussey, that developments in Britain reached a major turning point.

It is difficult to say whether Patrick Bell or Cyrus McCormick invented the first practical reaping machine, but it is known that the McCormick family had made attempts to construct a machine before 1831. Robert McCormick, father of Cyrus, was a farmer in Virginia, USA, and as early as 1816 he had made a machine to cut corn, but achieved little result. The younger McCormick took an interest in the problem and by the harvest of 1831 he was able to demonstrate successfully his own version of the reaper. It consisted of a low platform for collecting the corn, with an arrangement of blades for cutting the stalks positioned across the leading edge.

In the absence of money to develop the enterprise, progress was not easy for the McCormick family. They had become bankrupt as a result of another venture, but reports about the success of their machine had quickly travelled around the countryside. In 1840 their first reaper was sold, and by 1844 fifty had been dispatched.

McCormick took out a patent for an improved version in 1845. The angle of the cutting teeth was adjusted and a new device for separating the standing corn incorporated. Of the many reaping machines shown at the Great Exhibition, the American

McCormick and Hussey versions triumphed by reason of their simplicity, and both worked well in subsequent public and private trials. Having acquired such high reputations, they came into general use almost immediately. It was in the following year that Bell's reaper re-appeared to challenge the Americans. Basically it was the same as the machine that had been tried secretly in the closed barn, but it had some important alterations. The Hussey machine was completely defeated by Bell's when the two were put on trial at the Highland Society Show in 1852. A challenge was then issued to McCormick by the victorious Bell, but the contest did not take place until a year or so later, when again the premium was awarded to Bell.

British manufacturers had been full of enthusiasm upon seeing the two American machines, which sold in great numbers throughout the country, Hussey's machine being more favoured than McCormick's. In the following years several makers proceeded to exhibit reapers of their own design. Patents were taken out at a rapid pace, and the agricultural trials of the 1850's saw a great many machines in all stages of development. All were capable of proving their efficiency, but a reaping machine at a low price, suitable for the average farmer, was still something for the future.

The McCormick machine was improved by the addition of a Burgess and Key delivery mechanism, whereby the corn having been cut fell into a series of Archimedean Screw rollers which delivered a continuous and well-formed swath at the side of the machine. A similar side delivery system had been attached by Crosskills to Bell's reaping machine. This method of discharging the corn was to grow in favour over that of manually

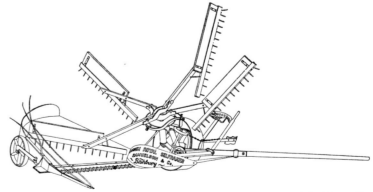

Samuelson's New Patent 'Omnium' Self-Raking Reaping Machine, 1877 (plate 9)

raking the machine clear, and McCormick added revolving rake arms to clear the cut grain from the platform of his reaper. In 1862 a similar type of raker was being used by Samuelson & Co, of Banbury, and this was to remain the accepted method for almost half a century.

Patrick Bell died in 1869 knowing that all his efforts had achieved the success he had wished for. He had received presentations and acknowledgements from his countrymen as the inventor of the first effective reaping machine. Cyrus McCormick died rather later, in 1884. He had become a rich man since the family had developed the International Harvester Company, and before the end of the century their Chicago factories were producing thousands of harvesters every week.

Sheaf-gathering mechanism was currently being perfected, and when the first sheaf binder was exhibited at Birmingham in 1876 it proved to be the final step in the development of the self-binder. By the end of the nineteenth century the main features of the reaper-binder had become firmly established. String had replaced wire for sheaf tying. The weight and draught of the machines had been reduced, and control levers were provided to adjust the reel and cutting platform positions. Farmers were still dubious about the merits of the reaper-binder, but it was accepted into general use before the First World War.

The first combines came into this country in 1928. British farmers were not enthusiastic, since American tractors brought here earlier had failed to work well in the damper English climate, and it was feared that the efficiency of the combines would be affected similarly. Despite the objections, however, the combine established its superiority and the number of machines in use increased rapidly every year.

SECTION 7

Threshing machinery

The earliest known method of threshing was to beat the grain from the ears of corn with a stick. The ancient Egyptians and Israelites improved on this by spreading out the loosened sheaves on hard ground and then driving oxen over them to tread out the grain. But this practice must inevitably have damaged a portion of the crop, and it was superseded by the threshing sledge. The Romans used such an implement as this, called the *tribulum*, consisting of a heavy wooden frame mounted on rollers, which was dragged over the piles of sheaves. It was, however, an improved construction of the threshing stick – the flail – that came into general use for threshing the lighter types of grain. The flail was made up of two sticks joined by an eelskin thong. The worker grasped one stick as a handle, then swinging the free part above his head, brought it down across the sheaves which were spread out on the ground. Although the method took up considerable time and labour of both men and animals, and the result had little to commend it since much of the grain was damaged and mixed with earth and grit, corn was still being threshed by flail at the end of the nineteenth century; and this notwithstanding that a mechanical thresher had long been available.

The origin of the threshing machine is obscure. It is known that little progress was achieved until 1786 when a successful thresher, not dissimilar in principle from the modern machine, was invented by Andrew Meikle, of East Lothian. This consisted of flails fixed to a beam, turned by a water-wheel. When demonstrated, it was shown that the machine could thresh far more grain from the stalks than could ever be done by hand flailing.

Other inventors had nevertheless been at work on the problem before Meikle. The first man to consider the idea of threshing grain by rubbing it between rollers instead of the flailing method was a Mr Ilderton who lived in Alnwick, Northumberland. His machine was made about 1776. It consisted of a large revolving drum around which were arranged a number of adjustable rollers, the function of which was to rub out the grain as the sheaves passed between them. A Scotsman, Sir Francis Kinlock, used the principle of Ilderton's machine but placed the drum inside a corrugated cover. Four adjustable pieces of wood were fixed to the outside of the revolving drum so that they pressed against the corrugated cover, thus rubbing out the grain as the sheaves passed through.

But most of the early machines were inefficient; bruising of the grain was the biggest fault. Nevertheless ideas and developments continued to flourish. There was a great deal of debate at this time among farmers, inventors and other interested parties about the merits of the powered flail compared with those of the rubbing machine. Indeed it is on record that Meikle spent considerable time trying to perfect the flail method before he considered the idea of using two fluted rollers between which the sheaves passed before being beaten by a revolving drum.

William Winlaw, an agricultural implement-maker, was encouraged by his employer to design and construct a threshing machine. His first two attempts failed to work, but he did achieve success in 1785 by using the idea of a conical rubbing mill. The ears of corn first had to be combed free from the straw by hand and then fed down a chute into the machine, where a spiral mill turned by gears from a handle separated the grains from the heads without any threshing at all.

In 1797 William Spencer Dix produced a machine that rubbed out the grain by means of a flat, grooved stone which rotated in a shallow wooden container. The corn was passed down from a hopper by two small fluted rollers.

Although during this time most of the threshing was being done by flail, research was going on in both England and Scotland to develop combined threshing and winnowing machines. In the final form of the thresher the incorporation of winnowing machinery became a vital part, but in the early years this adjunct was distinctly crude. Traditionally, winnowing and threshing were quite separate operations. The primitive method of winnowing the grain was to pile the trodden-out corn in a suitable place out in the open and to separate the corn from the admixture of short straw and chaff by throwing it up into the wind. This was the practice in countries where the weather was reliable, but in England the draught between the two open barn doors was utilised. Eventually the winnowing machine was developed to obviate the need for depending upon such currents of air. James Meikle, the father of Andrew, had probably seen such machines in Holland, and when he returned to Scotland he built a simple hand-operated machine incorporating four canvas sails which supplied the necessary draught.

By 1770 this first device had been much improved by James Sharp, who made a machine that cleaned and sorted the grain from the waste. This was of wooden construction and had an internal fan by which a blast of air blowing through sieves separated the grit and other impurities from the grain. The dust was blown out at the end, the clean wheat coming out of a screen at the side. This machine was highly praised by farmers in Yorkshire, and most of the larger farmers adopted it. The smaller farmers got together to buy a machine collectively. Most village carpenters made their own versions of the more primitive fanner, but canvas sails were being replaced by thin sheet metal, and by about 1796 nearly all farmers had winnowers of some description below their threshing machines.

By the end of the eighteenth century threshing machines driven by horse-power were fast coming into use in Scotland, though their acceptance in England was much slower. It was customary for the threshing to be done in a barn. Here the threshing device was placed on the upper floor and the grain, after having been beaten, was passed down through the winnowing machine to ground level free of chaff.

William Spencer Dix's Thresher, c 1790, from his *Remarks on Utility*, 1797

Until now, threshing machines had been static constructions, but by the turn of the century experiments were being undertaken to make them transportable. Thomas Wigful, of Norfolk, exhibited a wheeled machine at Woburn in 1803.

During the next twenty-five years threshing machines spread rapidly and eventually sparked off a farm labourers' revolt against them, since the feeling was widespread among workers that they would now be unemployed on wet days and during the winter months, when threshing was the customary job.

In 1848 Charles Burrell & Sons, of Thetford, Norfolk, made the first combined threshing and dressing machine. Improvements were encouraged over the following decade by the annual competitions, where manufacturers could exhibit and demonstrate their machines. By this time steam was being used as the motive power and reliable threshing machines were being manufactured and sold in great numbers. They had also become huge and complicated, and therefore manufacturers were striving to standardise and simplify the vast array of wheels, bearings and driving straps that the transportable threshing machine presented at this time. It was by far the most involved machine used by the farmer, and it was also very expensive to maintain; on the other hand, however, it was economical enough when hired out by a contractor.

All the latest improvements were on display in 1872, when competitions between manufacturers took place in order to find the best portable combined threshing and dressing machine. The construction of these machines was of heavy timber, trussed from top to bottom with wrought-iron diagonal straps, and all were suitable for being driven by a portable steam engine. The threshing drum was of iron and fitted with steel bearings. Oil-baths were provided on most bearings to reduce the danger of overheating. The iron concaves that rubbed the grain against the drum were sectional, so that after a few years' work they could be turned, and so present a new, sharp edge to the drum. Threshing and separation were perfected, corn and screenings were delivered into sacks at the rear of the machine, whilst straw and chaff were separated and discharged at the front.

The dangers involved in feeding the machine were reduced by the self-feed system, invented by a Mr Wilders, of Grantham. This feeder involved four reciprocating shakers which loosened out the sheaves and conveyed them to the threshing drum after the tying bands had been cut by hand. The whole system could be stopped instantly by a lever that threw the belt off the driving pulley at the side of the machine. A later development, the 'Invincible' self-feeder, was similar to Wilders' system but incorporated its own automatic band-cutter. Improvements were continually being made to the mechanism of the thresher. The tendency was to leave the framework more open than before, so that faults could be traced and repaired more easily.

An accessory to the threshing machine was the straw elevator, and those shown at the Royal Show in 1863 were considered by the judges to be crude in construction and too expensive for the average farmer. They were, however, a valuable item and subsequent research resulted in telescopic and folding frames, made of light metal, that could be extended well above the height of a rick and retracted compactly for transportation.

By the close of the nineteenth century harvest work had become fully mechanised. Machines were available for reaping and binding the crop, threshing, dressing and bagging the grain, and for elevating or stacking the straw into ricks.

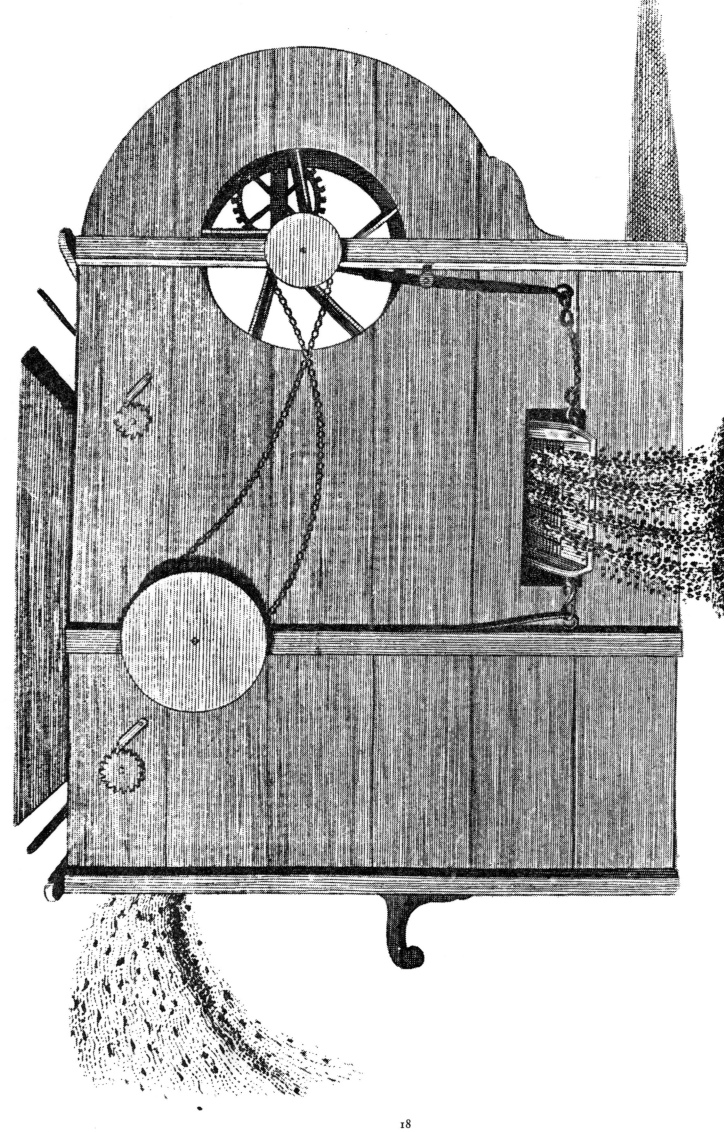

James Sharp's 'Winnowing Machine', c 1770, from *Agricola Sylvan Farmers Magazine*, 1772

SECTION 8

Fodder machines

It was not until late in the eighteenth century that machines for preparing animal foodstuffs were developed. Prior to this the food was either chopped or sliced by hand. A prize was offered by the Society for the Encouragement of the Arts in the early 1760's for a machine that would slice turnips and thus reduce the risk of animals choking themselves by swallowing roots whole. This competition produced a simple cutting box which cut and mixed the different items of food, and in this way animals were forced to take a certain amount of the poorer foodstuff along with the good. This aid to animal feeding was little more than a shallow container about 3 ft long by 6 in. wide and open along the top. Roots, hay and straw were fed into this box by the operator, who held the material secure by means of a piece of wood connected by chain to a treadle below. The protruding ends were then cut off close to the machine by a knife-edge lever.

Excellent mechanical chaff cutters of all makes and sizes were to be found by the mid-nineteenth century. The best of them had ribbed or studded rollers that gripped the straw and pushed it forward through a wheel fitted with two curved cutting knives.

The advantages of cutting up the animal foodstuff were now generally recognised, and machines for this purpose were becoming indispensable on the larger farms and also to the brewery and railway companies which used horses. By 1850 some implement manufacturers were offering a large steam-driven chaff cutter for use where large numbers of horses, sheep or cattle were being kept, and in spite of its huge, cumbersome appearance, this machine was basically quite simple as well as being reliable. Except for a wooden hopper it was made of metal and could be adjusted to cut three convenient sizes of chaff—3/16ths in., $\frac{1}{2}$ in. and $\frac{3}{4}$ in. The machine also had a safety device which would instantly arrest the rollers should the hand of the operator be drawn in. It was estimated to cut 30–35 cwt of half-inch chaff per hour.

A new machine for slicing turnips was demonstrated in 1820. This could be adapted to cut pieces of various sizes and was similar to the chaff cutter in its working principle. It was improved by the use of a hopper which held the roots and fed them (by their own weight) on to a series of rotating blades. With this machine the farmer was able to slice one bushel of roots per minute. A better version was Gardener's Turnip Slicer, which was to remain the most popular for the next quarter of a century.

Attempts were made to mount a similar machine on to a mobile cart, with the object of cutting and strewing the roots across the field in one continuous operation, the cutting knives being driven by a shaft from the cart-wheels. Machines were devised to cut and mix two kinds of roots simultaneously, and to cut them into flat slices or fingers. There was also a machine which pulped the roots or ground them into shreds.

In spite of the considerable developments in this type of farm machinery, primitive hand cutters remained popular, the simplest form being that of blades fixed into the end of a short wooden pole and used to strike and cut the roots as they lay on the ground. Another type was the hand-operated lever and block, in which by pulling the lever down and forcing the roots through a grid of sharp metal blades, sliced fodder fell into a container below.

By 1860 there were machines to split and crush beans, shell maize and crush oil cake. All the new developments were fostered by numerous agricultural competitions and displays and, as a result, defects were continually being remedied and designs and materials improved.

Portable steam engines

Despite the undoubted advantages of the use of steam, the exploitation of the steam engine as a source of power on farms was very limited. It took the form of a stationary engine fixed to the floor of a barn, where it drove various machines by means of belts and pulleys. Only the larger farms were able to afford it, but it was also frequently to be found installed in malt-houses and breweries. Accordingly manufacturers considered the idea of making the engine portable by mounting it on wheels – inspired no doubt by the railway engines of that period. To guide the engine whilst it was mobile, a team of horses had to be harnessed to a draw-bar fixed to the front axle. During the very early years of development the portable steam engine was pulled to the work where it was required entirely by the power of horses, but eventually only the steering was done by the horse, since the engine provided its own power to drive the wheels. Nevertheless these unwieldy but robust old engines solved the problem of mechanical threshing power on smaller farms, the majority of which could not afford to provide their own threshing plant.

Most of the larger manufacturers constructed a range of portable steam engines as an essential aid to their portable threshing machines. By the middle of the century the demand for both machines was increasing, and during the next decade achieved even greater proportions.

The small portable 2½ n.h.p. steam engine of this time, with 5½-in. cylinder and 8-in. stroke, was suitable for powering by means of its flywheel small steam threshing machines, grinders and crushing mills, chaff cutters, root pulpers and other farm machinery. For the heavier type of threshing machine a larger portable engine was available, from 3 to 12 n.h.p. with a single cylinder, and some with two cylinders from 10 to 30 n.h.p. These were also capable of driving heavy industrial machinery.

To keep pace with the continuous demand for greater fuel economy, manufacturers made the portable compound engine, which was provided with two cylinders – one high pressure and one low pressure. The steam maintained in the boiler was first of all admitted into the smaller or high pressure cylinder; then after being utilised there, instead of being allowed to escape it was fed into the larger low-pressure cylinder, where by further expansion it provided a considerable amount of extra power.

Ransomes, Sims & Jefferies Ltd fitted their portable engines with straw-burning apparatus of two types – the Head and Schemioths system and the Elworthy system. By means of these devices not only straw could be used as fuel for the engine but also reeds, small branches, brushwood or any similar material.

Using the Head and Schemioths system, the boiler was fitted with an extra large fire-box, and the apparatus for feeding in the straw was driven from the engine crankshaft by a belt. The device consisted of two rollers which were fixed at the fire-box door, together with a trough for conveying the straw to the rollers. The straw was driven into the fire-box in a 'fan' shape so

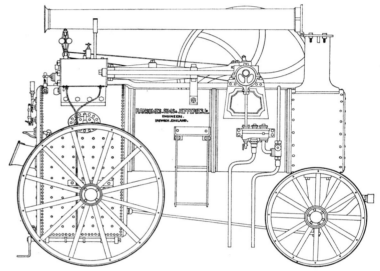

Ransomes, Sims & Jefferies Straw Burning Portable Engine, c 1900 (plate 5)

that each straw caught fire instantly. The rollers had to be turned by hand to raise the steam when work first started, but as soon as sufficient steam had been accumulated to start the engine the belt was affixed and the rollers were driven direct from the engine crankshaft. Only one man was needed to feed the straw into the fire-box, and by this method 8–10 sheaves of straw provided enough fuel to thresh 100 sheaves of wheat.

The discovery in various parts of the world of petroleum and other oils, which provided cheap and reliable engine fuel, induced manufacturers to adapt the boilers of their portable engines to take oil as readily as any other fuel.

A semi-portable engine was available for driving fixed threshing or barn machinery. It was exactly the same as the portable type in design, size and power, but it had no land-wheels. Instead it was mounted upon two pedestals, one of which stood under the fire-box and the other under the smoke-box.

It is impossible to give a date for the first occasion on which a plough was hauled by means of a steam engine, but it is certain that ploughing and hauling by steam were common enough by the mid-nineteenth century. An engraving from a publication of 1857 records a demonstration at Louth, Lincs, by a Burrell-Boydell engine which drew four double-breasted ploughs. Later in the century road steamers were frequently used for ploughing, and in the latter years steam traction-engine manufacturers could supply special crankshafts, counter shafts and main axles, of larger dimensions than usual, to adapt their machines to the stress of direct traction ploughing. The same firms also provided a wide range of gigantic cultivation implements for use with the steam traction-engine. But also at about this time the oil tractor made its appearance in the farming catalogues.

SECTION 10

John Fowler and the steam plough

The earliest patent of a steam ploughing apparatus was in the name of Major Pratt in 1811. His idea involved placing a portable steam engine in the centre of the field. The engine drove an endless 'rope' which turned around two movable anchor pulleys, and at each end of the field. Two ploughs were attached to the one rope hauled back and forth across the field between the engine and the anchors. There is no evidence to show if this method was ever put into practice, but it seems likely that the idea may have provoked later inventors to produce a similar apparatus that became popular towards the end of that century.

The next patent, taken out in 1812 by William and E. W. Chapman, was for a steam engine with a rigger, working on a stretched rope which was secured at both ends by movable anchors. The worst fault was found to be friction produced by the rope when in contact with the ground, and the proposed machine was soon abandoned. Nevertheless the rigger principle for plough haulage was adopted later and modified by many inventors.

Other patents quickly followed, but little practical success was achieved until John Heathcoat, Member of Parliament for Tiverton, obtained a patent in 1832 for an apparatus designed for bog reclamation. He was assisted in this enterprise by Josiah Parkes, well known at the time for his expert knowledge of agricultural drainage. The first trial of Heathcoat's invention took place four years after the date of the patent, and was held at Chat Moss, Lancashire. The engine employed a continuous track on both its sides and these tracks revolved on two large drums and four intermediate tension pulleys. The tracks were each 6 ft wide and the distance between the front and rear drums was 26 ft. This area (nearly 300 sq. ft) was necessary to give the buoyancy required whilst working on waterlogged soil.

Two anchored pulleys were placed each side of the engine at a distance of 250 yards, and the two ploughs operated simultaneously between the engine and the anchors. When working, the drag rope was wound off the drum positioned across the engine boiler, and passed to the opposite headland, around the anchor pulley and then returned to the engine, where it was fixed to the opposite end of the drum.

The plough carriage was fastened on to this endless rope and when the drum was put into motion one end of the rope coiled into the drum and the other end 'payed out'. The engine was gradually moved across the centre of the field and the two portable anchors moved across the headlands in the same direction, with the ploughs working continuously between the engine and their respective anchors. The ploughs, of single-furrow design, worked very well and were guided by one person, although the whole machinery set-up required the full attention of ten men. As meritorious as the machine and method seem to have been, the reclamation of bog-land was too specialised to arouse the interest it really deserved. It is not known why the inventor did not transfer his idea to ordinary cultivation, but had he done so he would no doubt have achieved excellent results.

Heathcoat was only one of the many inventors who lost money on their projects. Competition was encouraged by the Highland Society's prize of £500 offered for the first successful method of applying steam power to soil cultivation. Opinion at this time was very much divided between the merits of haulage by locomotive engines and that of rope haulage. Ideas on both systems continued to flourish, but very soon a Mr Hannam developed a highly successful system of cable ploughing that was used and perfected by Fowler.

The Marquis of Tweedale designed a similar system that was first used in 1857. The apparatus was made by Tullocks' and the system used two engines, just as Fowler's were doing about

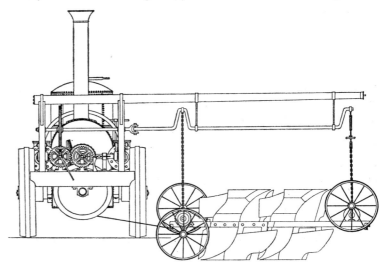

Marquis of Tweedale's Ploughing Engine, 1857 (plate 2)

this time. The front wheels could be turned and the drive was provided from the rear wheels. Two ploughing speeds, 3½ and 5 m.p.h., were provided. Tweedale thought it necessary to clear the land of flints and stubble before any steam ploughing took place, and it was for this purpose that he invented his horse-drawn subsoil plough.

When the plough came within a certain distance of the engine, it was lifted clear of the ground by means of a cranked shaft attached to the horizontal beam above the engine. This shaft was moved by engine power and the plough turned over on its axis. Another turn of the crankshaft lowered the plough and positioned it for the return run across the field. Whilst the plough was moving away the engine moved forward 56 in., which equalled the width of four 14-in. furrows. When it was moving on the highway the top fixtures and all the accessories were loaded on a wagon at the rear of the engine. Fully laden, the machine could achieve a speed of 4 m.p.h.

Other inventors associated with pioneer machines were John Osborne, Lord Willoughby d'Eresby and Fiskin. But the credit for complete success must go to John Fowler and the firm that he founded. It was whilst he was in Ireland during 1849 that Fowler first noticed large tracts of bog-land and from this impression conceived his initial ideas of large-scale drainage by mechanical methods. Together with Albert Fry, of Bristol, he built his first drain plough in the late 1840's and accepted a contract for the drainage of Hainault Forest in Essex.

In 1853 Fowler applied steam power to his draining plough, and the machine was shown at the Lincoln 'Royal' in the following year. The judges were very impressed, being of the opinion that if steam could be used successfully in this way, then it could be applied suitably to other farming techniques. Fowler accepted the challenge and attempted cultivation by steam in 1855. He abandoned any idea of locomotive diggers. Instead a stationary steam engine was employed to move the plough to and fro across the field on an endless wire rope. His experimental equipment was made by Ransomes and, together with Jeremiah Head, he developed a steam-ploughing set which won the Highland Society's long-offered prize of £500 at the Chester 'Royal' in 1858.

Fowler's plough consisted of two sets of plough-bodies attached to a long beam frame, four shares at one end pointing towards those at the other end, and all were balanced upon a centre axle and two large wheels. The operator rode upon the tail of the implement and guided it by altering the angle of the land-wheels through worm-and-rack steering. A combined engine and hauling drum was placed at one end of the field and a self-propelling anchor and pulley at the other. Both moved slowly across the headlands, so that they were always opposite, while the plough traversed up and down the land between them, hauled by the endless rope. Instead of coiling on to a barrel, the rope was held by being passed around grooves on a drum, so enabling the rope to bear a heavier load than when it was subjected to the jerking motion of being wound upon its own irregular coils. This grooved drum, set on a vertical axis and carried on a bracket frame underneath the boiler, was driven by toothed gearing and an upright shaft from the engine crankshaft. There were also two pulleys, one at each end of the boiler. Two three-quarter turns around the drum were sufficient to prevent the rope from slipping, even under the force of a ten- or twelve-horse engine. If any rock or other obstacle obstructed passage, the rope would slip in the grooves and prevent breakage. This was an important consideration, since a complete rope woven entirely of iron wire cost in the region of £40. Later a single steel wire was intertwined with the iron wire, and in 1857 all-steel ropes, which lasted four times as long as the iron ones, were introduced.

The wooden beams were made so as to adjust to any breadth of furrow, and for subsoil trenching Cotgreave Irons were supplied.

The same implement could be used as a scarifier by removing the ploughs and attaching a light frame fitted with tines. On reaching the end of the furrow the implement was prepared for the return journey without being turned, simply by pulling down the end of the suspended frame, then directing its course into the next line of work.

The engine was fitted with a pitch chain and the required gear to propel itself from field to field or along the highway, with a single horse in the shafts for steering.

The price of Fowler's steam ploughing apparatus in 1860 was:

Ten-horse engine (double-cylinder) with self-moving and reversing gear, windlass, water cart, anchor, 800 yards of steel rope, headland rope, 16 rope porters, two snatch-blocks and field tools: £622
Four-furrow ploughs with scarifier irons   81

Total cost £703

Fowler was constantly experimenting with the design of his engines, tackle and working systems. In 1860 he made a further improvement in his double-engine system, which was to become probably the most effective form of steam cultivation anywhere in the world. This system required the use of two engines arranged on opposite sides of the field, each having a winding drum. The engines acted alternately: one payed out the rope with a free drum and moved up the headland ready for the return of the implement as the other engine wound the rope in. The cost of all this complicated tackle was, of course, far too high for the average farmer, but steam-ploughing contractors were now emerging all over the country. Fowler's ceaseless activity was rewarded, since by the mid-1860's his Leeds factory was employing nearly 1,000 men; but the pace affected his health and he was forced to retire. He died in 1864 at the age of thirty-eight.

Many manufacturers were taking out patents for ploughing engines and steam ploughing apparatus about this time, but

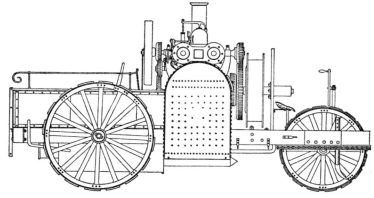

Howard's Improved Winding Engine, 1867 (plate 11)

although the idea of mounting the winding drums vertically had been considered much earlier, it was not until 1879 that it was incorporated in a patent by Everest and Adams.

In 1863 the Howard Brothers constructed a vertical-drum engine which was carried by a three-wheeled chassis. By using two of these engines, placed on opposite headlands, they developed a system of cultivation whereby each worked one-half of a field. It was an ungainly machine that could never be described as a traction-engine, and when it was modified in 1867 the resulting design, though functional, was again most unimaginative. It was capable of hauling up to 30 tons. Howards replaced this machine in 1874 with a much improved model on the lines of the traditional traction-engine.

FOWLER'S PATENT STEAM PLOUGHING APPARATUS,

which is fully described on page 30 of this Catalogue, and to which the following PRIZES have been awarded :—

The **GOLD MEDAL** at the French Exhibition, in 1856.

The **Highland Society's PRIZE** of £200, at Stirling, 1857.

The **Royal Agricultural Society's PRIZE** of £500, at the Chester Meeting, 1858.

The **Yorkshire Agricultural Society's PRIZE** of £50, at Northallerton, 1858.

Lord Bolton's PRIZE of £25, at Northallerton, 1858.

The **Royal Agricultural Improvement Society of Ireland's PRIZE** of £50, at Londonderry, 1858.

The **Scotch Farmers' PRIZE** of £50, at Stirling, 1858.

The **Royal Agricultural Society's PRIZE** of £50 at Warwick, 1859.

The **Agricultural Society's PRIZE** of £50 at Ashford, 1859.

The **Royal Agricultural Society's PRIZE** of £90 at the Canterbury Meeting, 1860.

MAKING A TOTAL OF

£1065 IN PRIZES.

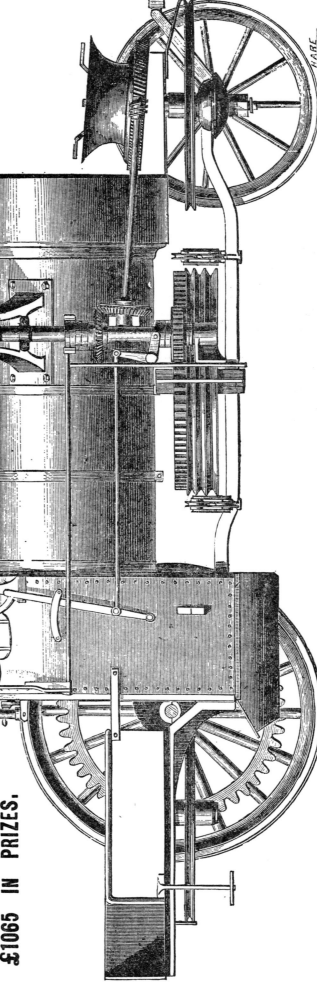

ENGRAVING OF A STANDARD SET OF COMBINED ENGINE AND WINDLASS GEAR WITH SELF-MOVING APPARATUS.

SECTION 11

Rotary digging machines

The nineteenth century saw many ingenious attempts at the perfection of rotary digging implements. The problem of mechanical cultivation fascinated a great number of inventors, many of whom had never before been concerned with agriculture, and it was probably for this reason that the majority of the ideas were more fantastic than practical.

Roberts' patent digging machine was the first of the many that evolved. It was patented in 1822, and comprised a large wheel with curved tines around the circumference. The wheel, set within a heavy chassis, was lowered into a hole previously dug by hand to the required depth. The wheel revolved and the tines extracted the soil as the whole machine was moved forward; it was probably hauled by capstan and horses.

An interesting adaptation of the plough resulted from the combined efforts of Thomas Bonsor and William Pettit in 1846. This was a screw plough which had a revolving axis fitted with cutting blades and positioned so as to replace the mouldboard. When hauled across a field by steam-cable the screw device rotated and cut a deep channel into the earth. It is unlikely that any of these plans were taken beyond the experimental stage, but the idea of the screw plough emerged later in Beauclerk's Archimedean subsoil plough, which was patented in 1850.

This implement was probably much smaller than the plough constructed by Bonsor and Pettit, since it was of a scale that could be worked with a pair of horses. Nevertheless the principle was the same. It was equipped with two wide iron wheels at the front to regulate the depth, and the subsoiling work was effected by three curved steel blades so placed on an axis, fitted into the underside plough frame, as to form a triple screw – rather like a ship's propeller. When the plough was drawn forward, the resistance of the soil caused the axis to rotate.

James Usher's 'steam plough', made in 1849, was the first important digging machine. This was to prove highly efficient, but it was expensive and therefore beyond the reach of all but the wealthiest farmers. It cost £300, weighed 5 tons and could plough to a breadth of 4 ft 2 in. and move the soil to a depth of 9 in. In its form it was similar to that of the portable steam engine, with the boiler mounted on a steel chassis. It was carried on a pair of wide rollers; the rear roller provided the drive and the front roller the steerage. Duplex cylinders supplied the motive power, transmitted by toothed gearing to the drive roller and to a horizontal transverse shaft equipped with curved mouldboards and shares supported by a lever frame at the rear of the machine. Fixed on to the shaft were five discs, each having three curved shares placed so that no two shares touched the ground simultaneously. The shares were made to rotate and penetrate the soil in the opposite direction to that in which the machine moved. The working depth could be varied by means of the adjustable frame.

A similar type of rotary tilling machine was made soon after-wards by Thomas Rickett, of the Castle Foundry, Buckingham. The rollers on Usher's machine were replaced by wide wheels, but again the power was transmitted by gearing from Duplex cylinders. The digger was driven by a chain from the engine crankshaft and involved the use of spiral shares, positioned horizontally across the rear of the machine. This implement was claimed to be capable of turning the soil to a width of 7½ ft, but it is doubtful if it ever reached a practical stage.

An elaborate, costly, but inspired invention was the 'Guideway System' developed by Lieut. Halkett, R.N. This method of cultivation needed the installation of iron rails, similar to a railway track, across the land at intervals of 50 ft. Two steam engines running on parallel rails carried a light girder type of bridging structure suspended between them well above ground level. The engines moved down the entire length of the tracks with various implements attached to the underside of the 'bridge'. When a 50 ft stretch of land had been completed, the whole apparatus, plus engines, were moved by means of link rails to bridge another section. The actual working costs were said to be not more than a few pence per acre.

The first Romaine digger (patented by Robert Romaine, of Peterborough, Canada) was constructed in 1853. The expense was borne by Alderman John Joseph Mechi, of Tiptree Hall, Essex. This horse-drawn machine was carried on wide wheels and had a lever frame at the rear which supported a steam-driven, cast-iron cylinder armed with curved digging tines. A second version of the machine was made in Canada and was shown at the Paris Exhibition of 1855. There it was seen by William Crosskill, of Beverley, Yorkshire, who was already an established maker of agricultural implements and steam engines. Crosskill undertook to improve upon Romaine's idea, and in 1857 the Romaine-Crosskill digger was produced. This had a Duplex cylinder 14 n.h.p. horizontal engine that powered both travelling wheels and digging cylinder. The weight of the machine was again carried on wide wheels, and the steering was effected by a pair of smaller castor-type wheels at the front. The cultivating section, at the front, remained much the same in principle, and it could dig a strip of soil 6½ ft wide to a depth of 12 in. The large driving wheels could each be put out of gear to enable the whole machine to turn in the smallest possible arc.

Smith's gang plough of 1861 was an idea based on the use of continuous tracks. A number of plates were joined together and ran as a track on each side of the machine. The working power was transmitted from a vertical boiler and Duplex cylinders to large driving wheels – one in the centre of each side. The two continuous tracks were moved by these wheels and they ran almost to the ends of the machine, where they turned on tension pulleys. The boiler and engine were carried on a heavy wooden platform with seven plough-shares fixed in horizontal beams across the front and rear ends. The balance of the machine could be tipped at the point of the large centre wheels, so that the entire weight could be applied to the set of shares that worked the soil. Steering was done by putting one track into neutral gear – a device that enabled the machine to be turned almost within its own length and so save waste at the headlands.

The first in a series of efficient and spectacular digging machines was designed by Thomas Churchman Darby, of Pleshy, Essex, in 1877. Between this time and 1898 thirty of these 20-ton machines, each costing £1,200, were manufactured by W. & S. Eddington, of Chelmsford, under the direction of Mr Darby. The complete digger took the form of a single-cylinder engine on top of a horizontal boiler, with geared drive to the 3½-ft diameter travelling wheels. The digging frames, comprising 41 tines in three separate sets and able to work to a width of 20 ft, were driven from the engine. Steering was provided through eight small wheels on a chassis projecting from the rear, and the whole could be controlled by a hand-wheel from the footplate. When the machine was digging the travelling wheels were in line parallel with the engine and boiler, but they had to be turned through 90 degrees when travelling on the road.

The Darby-Savage machine, which was later made at King's Lynn under Mr Darby's supervision, embodied modifications suggested by experience, although in general appearance it was much the same. The digging tines were formed into six individual frames and, by the use of a hydraulic jack, the whole weight of the machine could be lifted from the axles whilst the position of the wheels was altered.

A number of more manageable diggers, such as the Colchester, Cooper and Burrell-Proctor machines, were developed, but all took the form of 'digging' tines placed at the rear of a traction engine. As interesting as these attempts were, the chief drawback in farming operation was still the great weight of the machines and the consequential compacting of the soil.

The use of ordinary cultivating implements drawn by the lighter oil tractor came into favour during the early years of the twentieth century. But the evolution of the digging machine had justified itself, since it was eventually to be of great use to the excavating and road building contractor. The idea of rotary tillage was not abandoned entirely by the implement manu-facturers, but in 1893 McLarens had expressed the opinion that the plough would always be a more efficient means of cultivation than any rotary tillage machine.

The final phases in agricultural digging came in 1927 when Fowlers produced a 23-ton, 225-h.p. gyro-tiller which moved the soil to a depth of 20 in. A movable frame extended from the rear of this huge caterpillar tractor and carried two rings of 'shares' which rotated on a vertical axis. Further development led Fowlers into the production of an 80 h.p. gyro-tiller in 1930, together with the 'tractiller' which, although similar in principle, had to be drawn by tractor.

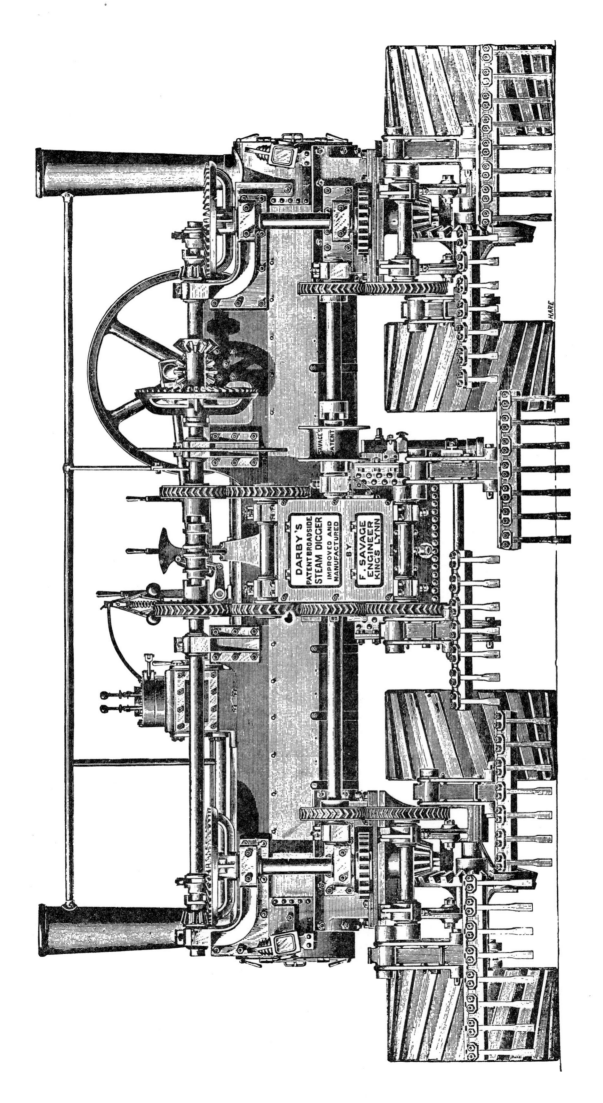

Darby-Savage Digger, c 1880

27

Early motor tractors

By the close of the nineteenth century it was becoming increasingly obvious that the future of farm power would rest very largely with the oil engine. Since Richard Hornsby and Sons, of Grantham, had started to manufacture their Hornsby-Ackroid patent oil engine in 1891, supported by a series of oil-engine trials for motor tractors held by the Royal Agricultural Society at Cambridge, the prospects opened to farmers, small as well as large, appeared to be limitless. Here was an efficient, clean method of powering all forms of barn machinery and providing a mobility in the field hitherto unknown.

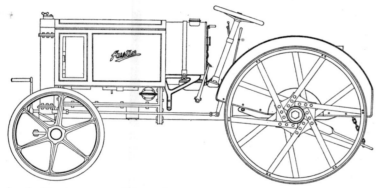

Austin Tractor, c 1920 (plate 13)

Hornsby and Sons produced their 18-b.h.p. oil-engine traction (or agricultural) locomotive in 1897, a machine that was capable of both road haulage and the powering of barn machinery. A similar development was taking place concurrently in the United States of America. The British tractor industry, pioneered by Ivel Agricultural Motors Ltd, started up on a large scale in 1902, and during the following twenty years produced some 900 tractors. The Ivel was a twin-engined machine, with a single lever adjustment for neutral, forward and reverse gears, provided by a huge cone clutch. The rear wheels were chain-driven and the tractor able to develop 24 b.h.p.

Ransomes, Sims & Jefferies, of Ipswich, exhibited their first petrol-motor tractor in 1903, but the project was abandoned within a year or so. This had been intended as a dual-purpose machine, capable of hauling implements or powering threshing and barn machinery. It had a friction clutch with three forward speeds and chain-driven rear wheels powered by a four-cylinder, 20-h.p. engine. Later, Ransomes offered a larger tractor which could be run on either oil or paraffin. Because of its size – 18½ ft long, 7 ft 2 in. wide and 10 ft 10 in. to the top of the chimney and weighing 10 tons – it was conceived primarily as an agricultural tractor suitable for driving a threshing machine and other farm machinery. It was also capable of hauling the thresher from farm to farm, and equally useful for light haulage and direct traction ploughing when the land was in a suitable condition. Its main advantage was that it could be run on low-grade

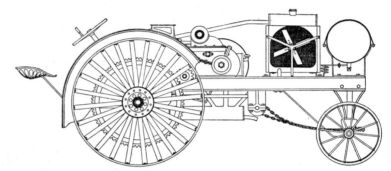

Overtime Tractor, 1917 (plate 14)

oils. No carburettor was required, since a governor controlled the fuel inlet valve. The control was from the footplate by means of two levers: one controlled the belt which drove the clutch and brake, and the other controlled the speeds.

The idea of using endless tracks as platforms for vehicles had been discussed and illustrated as early as 1825, but it was not until 1909 that a tractor was made which employed the principle of a continuous chain of plate powered by a twin oil engine. It was made by Hornsby and Sons as a development of their earlier effort of building a similar steam-driven machine for military purposes. But such little interest was shown in this caterpillar type of tractor that the venture became a financial loss and in 1912 Hornsby sold the rights of the invention to Holt Manufacturing Co, of Stockton, California.

Around this time and up to the outbreak of the First World War some notable tractors were developed. In 1907 Blackstone & Co introduced their oil traction engine. In 1909 the Cyclone tractor made its appearance, also the Sanderson & Mills Universal. But in spite of the advantages of the motor tractor,

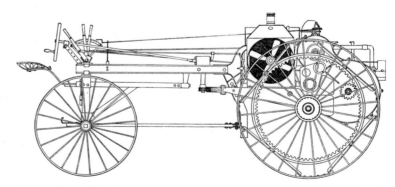

Moline Motor Plough, 1917 (plate 15)

farmers were still reluctant to accept it, mainly because of the high initial cost and the fear of having inflammable fuels around the farm.

To begin with, it was customary to use the tractor for ploughing and harrowing only, but grass mowers and binders were soon adapted for tractor haulage. Various types of draw-bars were manufactured, enabling four or five binders to be fixed to the rear of a single machine. The Universal model 'S' hauled five binders with ease.

It was the 1914–18 war that helped the development and ultimate perfection of the tractor. Greater and greater quantities of home-grown foodstuffs had to be produced as the war went on and the German submarine menace reduced imports to a trickle; at the same time farm workers were being called for military service, leaving the farms very much under-manned. After an attempt by a department of the British government to build a tractor in the early days of the war, an order for 7,000 Fordson machines was sent to the United States.

At the beginning of the war the boon type plough had been introduced, but this was little more than a plough with a driving motor attached. In this machine the number of cylinders varied from one to six, but it had two large driving and steering wheels at the front and smaller trailing wheels at the rear. One of the front wheels ran in the furrow, so requiring little steering of the machine. The plough formed one unit with the motor and in some cases could be lifted mechanically by means of a clutch on the land-wheels. The body of the plough could also be removed and various cultivating implements attached; a belt pulley was usually provided for driving light machinery.

At the Highland Agricultural Society's trial in 1917 it was evident that tractor design was at last beginning to form its own line. Machines were becoming much lighter and less likely to compact the soil. Considerable attention was also being given to the shape and size of the wheels. Demonstrations clearly proved that a light machine with adequate power could be an efficient aid to any farmer for ploughing, harvesting or the lighter forms of cultivation, such as seeding and harrowing.

Notwithstanding the flow of American tractors across the Atlantic, the war years stimulated many British ideas and developments. Notable amongst home-produced machines were the 'Ideal', with mechanism for direct powering to the reaper-binder attachment, and the Austin Culti-tractor, a 20-h.p., four-cylinder, three-wheel machine of 35 cwt.

By 1919 an extensive range of British and foreign motor tractors was available. To help small farmers choose machinery for their individual needs, the Society of Motor Manufacturers and Traders combined with the National Farmers' Union to stage a four-day exhibition and trial of tractors at South Carlton, Lincs, in September of that year. Another competition, again in Lincolnshire, was held in 1920 and was marked by the very high number of entries. Engines within the various models differed enormously, from the single-, double- and four-cylinder vertical engines to the single- and double-cylinder horizontal engines. The manufacturers of each claimed superiority in performance over the rest, with the most forceful advertising coming from the American firms. The most popular models in the 1920s were, however, either two-cylinder horizontal engines developing 500 r.p.m. or four-cylinder vertical engines at 1,000 r.p.m.

Steering on the early lightweight tractors was by a hand column direct to the front wheel through a gear-box; the heavier tractors had chain barrel steering, similar to that on the early steam engines.

Until diesel oil was used the fuel was paraffin, but the engine had to be started and run for a while on petrol until it was hot. To facilitate an explosive mixture, many machines had arrangements for heating the paraffin or air prior to its reaching the carburettor. This usually took the form of a feed-pipe coiled round the hot exhaust. Various arrangements to clean the intake air were fitted to these early machines. Some makers utilised a water-bath, through which all the indrawn air was taken, but the most common was a high chimney containing a dry filter-box.

Worm-driven gears were now rapidly ousting the chain drive, and differential and reverse gears were becoming standard features. A wary eye had to be kept on the American innovations in gears and steering, since the machines which were designed for flat prairie land were not always suitable for British conditions. Wheel and weight displacement, thickness of wheel rims and width of machines remained a controversial topic with both manufacturer and farmer, especially in regard to practicability when ploughing; in particular, difficulty was found in placing the tractor wheels in such a position as to satisfy the ploughman completely. Nevertheless, farmers were fully aware of the potential of this multi-purpose machine, since for a now moderate outlay it provided all the power necessary for the day-to-day running of a farm in both the yard and the field. Nearly all the early tractors were fitted with a belt pulley which, when not required for barn machinery, was capable of powering the threshing machine with almost the same efficiency as the steam traction engine. The most convenient position for the pulley was found to be on the side of the engine, and not, as in some makes, placed across the front or rear end of the machine. When placed at the side it was easier to manoeuvre the tractor backwards or forwards in order to put a suitable tension on to the belt. The main fault, however, lay in the fact that the pulley was small and therefore revolved too quickly, with the result that the belt was thrown off far too frequently.

During the early years of the motor tractor the farmer had to adapt his existing horse-drawn implements and vehicles to suit the newly acquired machine. Draw-bars to replace the shafts were usually constructed by the local blacksmith, but eventually manufacturers developed a wide range of towing attachments to convert most machines.

Many of the leading manufacturers who had previously made

implements for use with the steam-driven tractors used their experience to develop ploughs, harrows, cultivators, etc specially for the light motor tractor. One such implement was the disc harrow designed for cultivating rough land preparatory to making the seedbed. It had a 'T'-shaped chassis approximately 8 ft wide which held either 16 plain or 16 cut-away discs, usually of 18-in. diameter. Plain discs were preferred for general cultivation and cut-away discs for dry, hard land; and, as an added convenience, they were interchangeable. A similar implement was the double gang harrow, which had a row of spade-shaped blades followed by a row of discs. Trailers, such as forage-boxes and manure spreaders, designed specifically for attachment to the tractor, were not made until much later.

The design of ploughs for tractor attachment varied enormously, but could be divided into two basic types:

1. There was the independent plough, under complete control of the operator seated on it, and where the furrows, land- and hind-wheels were all controlled by separate levers.

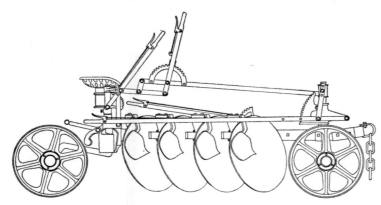

Ransomes, Sims & Jefferies Four-Furrow 'Key-Conqueror' Disc Plough, 1919 (plate 12)

2. The second type was the self-lift plough, which could be controlled easily by the tractor-driver from his seat. The lifting mechanism consisted of a toothed rack that was made to engage with a pinion fixed to the nave of the land-wheel. By throwing the lever forward the tractor-driver could cause the plough to climb gradually out of the work and be held securely in position until it was released. This arrangement was recommended in cases where the tractor was of Wallis, Austin, Fordson or Fiat types, with the lever readily accessible from the driving seat. If the tractor seat was placed away from the rear end of the machine, a cord lift was supplied.

A third type was the boon tractor and plough, in which motor and implement formed a single unit. A seat was usually provided for the operator, but he could walk alongisde if necessary.

BIBLIOGRAPHY

Clark, R. H., *The Development of the English Traction Engine*, Goose and Son, Norwich 1960.
Dickson's Practical Agriculture, 1805.
Donaldson, J., *British Agriculture*, 1860.
Fussell, G. E., *The Farmers' Tools*, Andrew Melrose, London, 1952.
Wright, Philip, *Old Farm Tractors*, Adam and Charles Black, London, 1962.

The Colour Plates

Mann's Reaping Machine, c1830

Marquis of Tweedale's Ploughing Engine. 1857

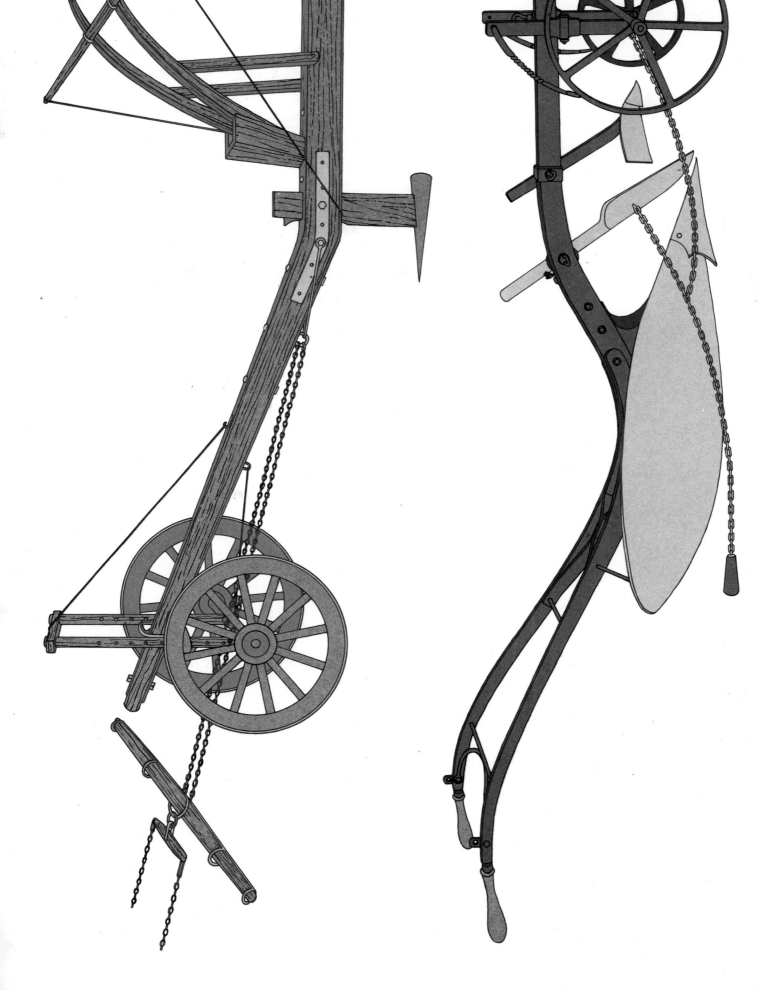

(top) Mr Vaisey's Mole Plough, c 1790

(below) Warwickshire Prize Plough, c 1850

Drawn by Michael Partridge   © A Hugh Evelyn Print

Jethro Tull's Drill, c 1700

Ransomes, Sims and Jefferies Straw Burning Portable Engine, c 1900

RANSOMES, SIMS & JEFFERIES LD.
ENGINEERS.
IPSWICH, ENGLAND.

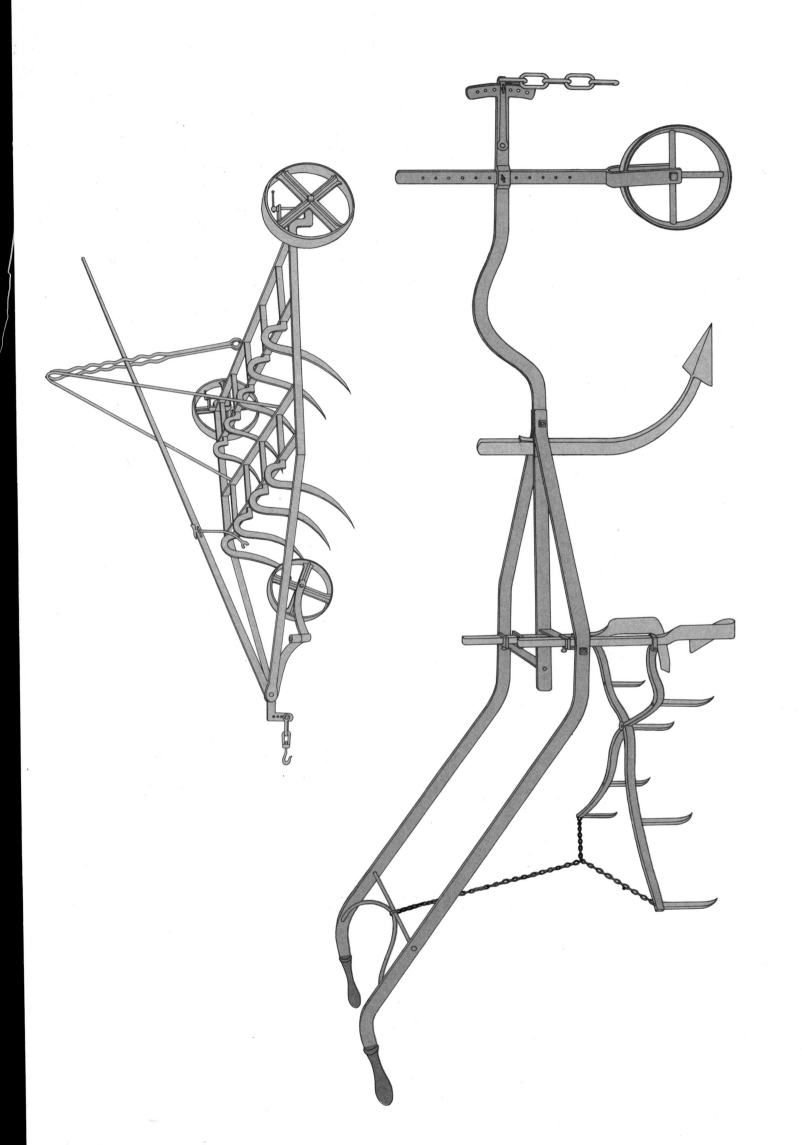

Horse Drawn Hoes, c 1860

Drawn by Michael Partridge © A Hugh Evelyn Print

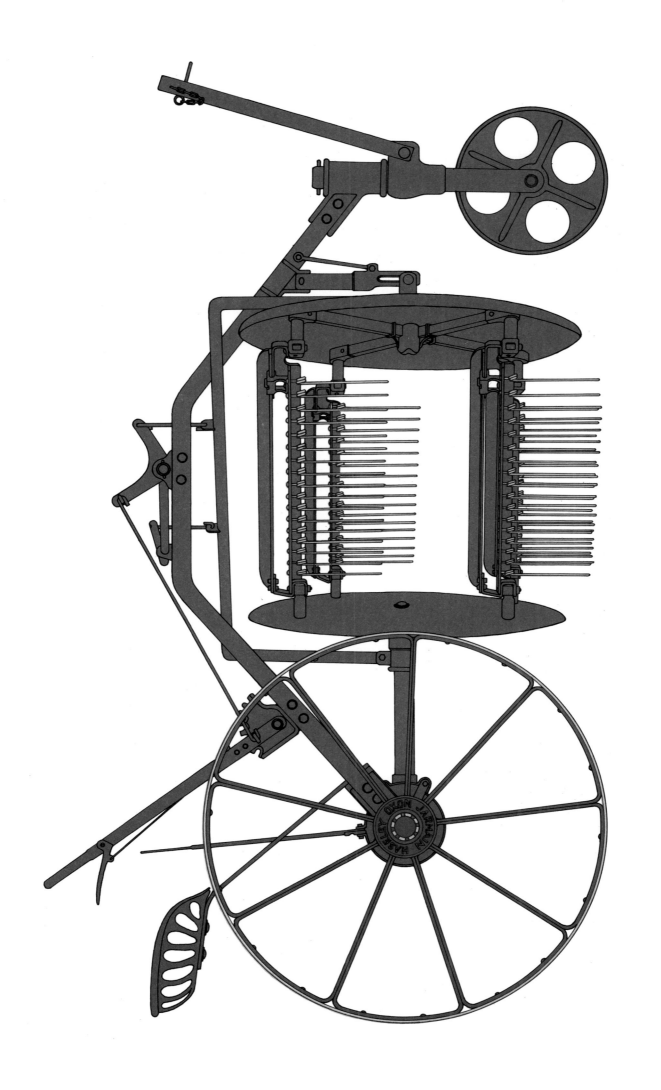

Combined Swath Turner and Side Delivery Rake, Jarmain, c 1920

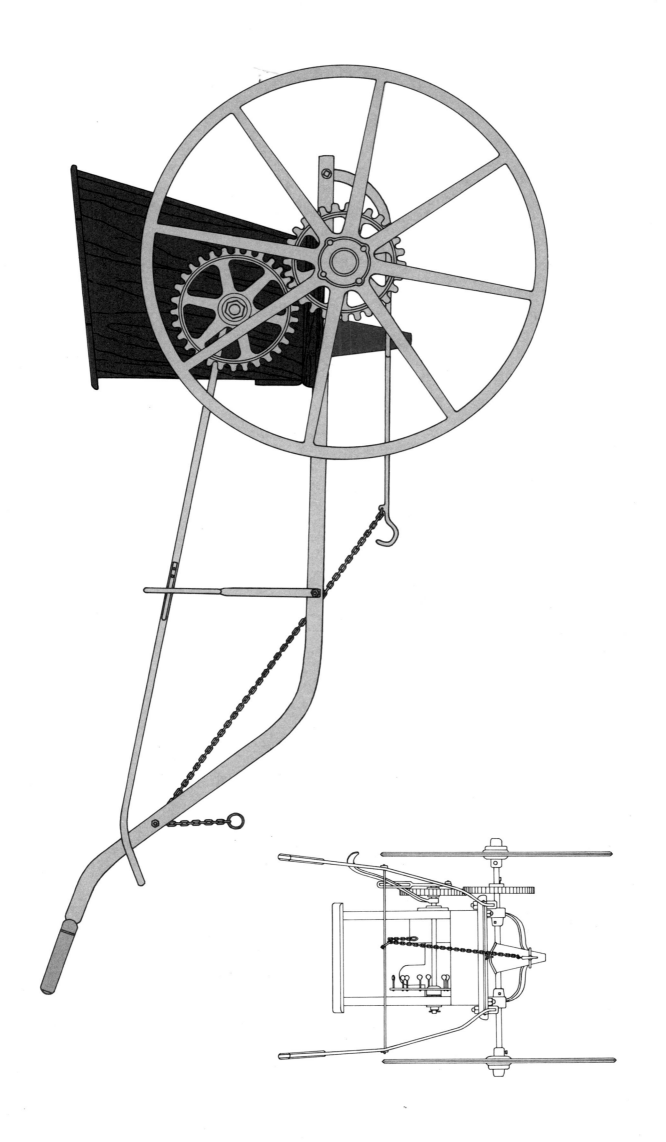

One-Row Seed Drill, c 1900

ROYAL SELFRAKER
SAMUELSON & Co.
~ Banbury ~

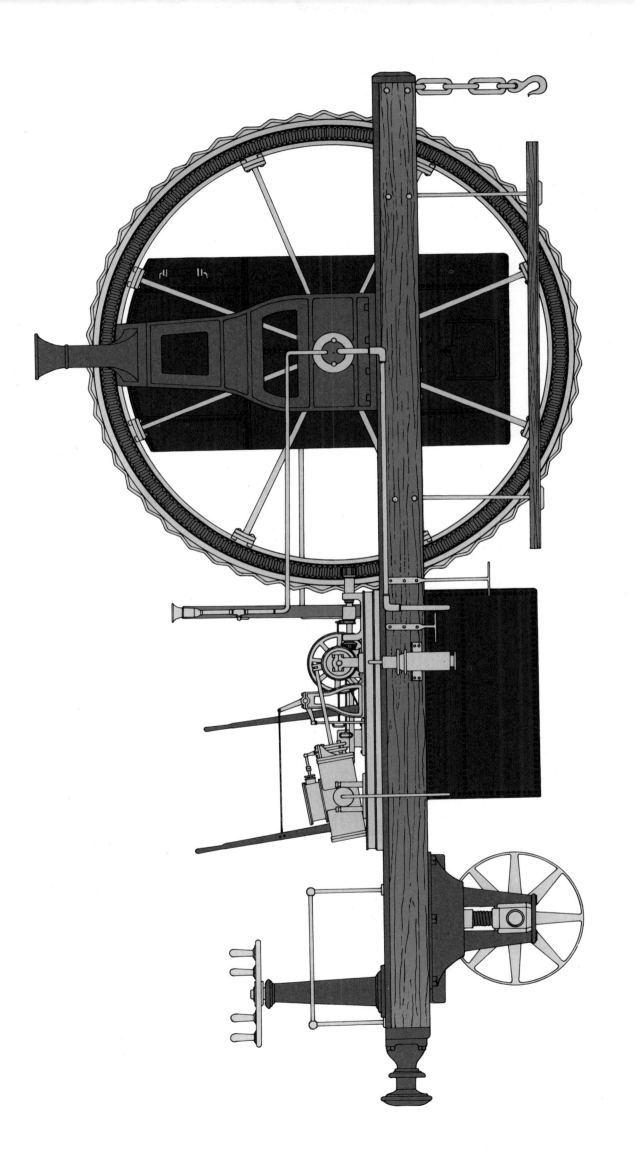

Blackburn Digger, 1857

Howard's Improved Winding Engine, 1867

Ransomes, Sims and Jefferies, Four-Furrow 'Key-Conqueror' Disc Plough, 1919

Drawn by Michael Partridge   © A Hugh Evelyn Print

Austin Tractor, c 1920

Overtime Tractor, 1917

Moline Motor Plough, 1917

(top) Ransomes, Head and Jefferies, Patent Double Plough with Subsoiler, c 1870

(below) Cuthbert Clarke's Draining Plough. c 1760

wn by Michael Partridge   © A Hugh Evelyn Print